The Innkeeper's Daughter

The Nativity as seen through a Young Girl's Eyes

by

Laura Thompson

MOORLEY'S Print & Publishing

© Copyright 1994

Unlike many play publishers we do not ask for any "Performing Rights" Royalties for this play but remind you that it is illegal to make copies of any part of this publication; by writing, printing, duplicating or photocopying without the Publisher's written permission.

ISBN 0 86071 430 6

MOORLEY'S Print & Publishing
23 Park Rd., Ilkeston, Derbys DE7 5DA
Tel/Fax: (0115) 932 0643

CAST

NARRATOR

MOTHER

FATHER

TRAVELLER

ESTHER

1st SHEPHERD

2nd SHEPHERD

1st KING

2nd KING

3rd KING

The Innkeeper's Daughter

NARRATOR: *Our story today revolves round this girl,*
So young and so neat and so pretty.
Esther's her name, and she lives at the inn
With her parents in Bethlehem City.

Now Esther's a good girl and works very hard
To give weary travellers rest.
But everyone's grumbling and whingeing today,
Although she is doing her best.

MOTHER: "Esther, come here and fold blankets with me.
We've got some fine guests here to stay.
Just look at the mess on the floor of this room!
You'll have to work harder today."

FATHER: "Esther, where are you? I need you in here.
These tables have got to be set.
Good gracious, my girl, you are terribly slow!
Haven't you finished that yet?"

NARRATOR: *Poor Esther is rushed off her feet all day long*
It's her job to answer the door.
Rat tat, rat-a-tat goes the knocker again.
And here comes one traveller more.

TRAVELLER: "My dear child, we've come to be taxed in this town.
Night falls, and your inn we espied.
O please say that you have a small room to spare
And let me and my wife come inside."

NARRATOR: *She said,*

ESTHER: "You can have the last room in the inn."

NARRATOR: *And with that gave the oak door a pull.*

ESTHER: "We've crammed such a lot of folk in here today
And now every last inch is full."

NARRATOR: *She made up the bed for the last of the guests.*
She was weary and ready to drop.
At last all her tasks for the day were complete,
But a sound just outside made her stop.

She then heard her father say to a man:

FATHER: "There's no room in this inn for the night.
I truly am sorry; my heart bleeds for you
To see you in such a great plight."

NARRATOR: *Now Esther was just a bit nosy, it's true*
And she peeped through the door with one eye.
Such a sad sight did she see through the gap
That she felt she was going to cry.

A young woman, soon to give birth to a child,
Was looking around in dismay,
And Esther, in pity, cried out to her dad,

ESTHER: "Why not let them both sleep in the hay?"

"There's room with the oxen and cows in the stall.
Although it is humble it's clean.
You can't send that poor young woman away.
O father, you can't be that mean!"

NARRATOR: *So Esther led Mary and Joseph straightway*
To lie down with the cattle and sheep.
Then she went to her bed and before very long
She had fallen into a deep sleep.

What strange dreams she had, as she
    slept through the night.
There were angels announcing a birth,
Singing,

ANGELS: "Glory to God in the highest
And peace to all men on the earth."

NARRATOR: *She awoke to find it was not just a dream.*
The angels were really on high,
And a brilliant star shining right overhead
Had lit up the whole of the sky.

She crept out of bed and put on her shawl
And went through the creaking inn gate,
Then down to the stable and in through the door.
She hoped she had not come too late.

For she felt, in her bones, something wondrous
she'd find.
In silence she gazed there in awe,
At the tiny new baby so snug and so warm
In a manger lined only with straw.

Esther was first to see the new child,
But soon she was joined in that place
By shepherds who'd come rushing down
from the hills,
Each one with great joy in his face.

1st SHEPHERD: "We were doing our job, watching over our flocks,
When the lights in the sky made us fear,
For our own lives and those of the sheep in our care
Till an angel spoke out loud and clear."

NARRATOR: *He said,*

ANGEL: "Go down now into Bethlehem City,
Go quickly before it is dawn.
There you will find, in a stable most humble,
The Lord Jesus Christ has been born."

2nd SHEPHERD: "So we left all our sheep on the hillside, in haste.
We followed the path by the light of a star,
Till we came to this place, in the night, and we've come,
Without gifts - just poor shepherds we are."

NARRATOR: *The shepherds and Esther knelt down by the babe,*
His mother and father stood by.
Then, back to their flocks the shepherds returned,
Their path lit, underneath the bright sky.

What was that noise out there in the yard?
Was it the shepherds come back?
No, there were three men on camels, outside
Who, clearly, of cash had no lack.

Their robes were of silk and of velvet, all jewelled,
And their trappings were silver and gold.

KINGS: "Where is the baby who's born to be king,
Whose birth, in our lands, was foretold?

We've looked for a palace, we've looked for rich folk,
We've dutif'lly followed a star.
We've travelled by night and we've travelled by day
And we've come from three countries afar."

NARRATOR: *Esther's eyes then lit up with great joy at these words.*

ESTHER: "No don't turn your camels around
And continue to travel away from this inn,
For the king that you sought has been found."

NARRATOR: *She led the three kings to the manger, and there*
They fell down and worshipped their king.
Unlike the poor shepherds, who had nothing to spare,
They each had a present to bring.

1st KING: "I bring him gold, worthy of his great rank."

2nd KING: "And frankincense, as he's divine."

3rd KING: "And myrrh, bitter sweet, I lay at his feet."

ALL TOGETHER: "These three gifts of kingship are thine."

NARRATOR: *"When you find the king, come and tell me soon*
So that I can worship him too,"

Herod had said, but the kings had been warned
That Herod's words were not true.

So the three kings set out on their long
   journey home.
They voted to go a new way.
Though Herod expected some news from them soon,
His bidding they would not obey.

It was near morning when Esther crept back
To her bed, and fell into a sleep.
She dreamed of a King, of a Saviour and Lord,
Who had a great promise to keep.

MOTHER: "Wake up, Esther do. It's time to start work.
This girl has no idea at all
Of what goes on in this inn every day.
Our guests are beginning to call!"

FATHER: "Where is that girl? There is breakfast to get,
And setting and clearing the table,
And I bet it hasn't entered your head
To see to those folk in the stable."

NARRATOR: *At this Esther smiled a knowing smile.*
She kept all these things in her heart.
Her parents would never believe what she'd seen,
And that she, too, had taken a part.

Was it only last night she had worshipped a king
In the lowly cattle's stall,
In the presence of shepherds and three fine kings?

ESTHER: "Yes, mother, did you call?"

MOTHER: "The trouble with you is you daydream, my girl.
You'll miss something crucial one day.
How can we ever trust you to care
For the guests who come to stay!"

NARRATOR: *"There would never be a guest such as him,"
Thought Esther as she dressed.*

ESTHER: "Of all the serving girls in this land
I must be the most truly blessed."

NARRATOR: *She smiled as she worked at the hardest of chores,
She hummed as she did everything.
For Esther, the innkeeper's daughter
Had knelt at the feet of a king.*

MOORLEY'S are growing Publishers, adding several new titles to our list each year. We also undertake private publications and commissioned works.

Our range of publications includes: **Books of Verse**
- Devotional Poetry
- Recitations

Drama
- Bible Plays
- Sketches
- Nativity Plays
- Passiontide Plays
- Easter Plays
- Demonstrations

Resource Books
- Assembly Material
- Songs & Musicals
- Children's Addresses
- Prayers & Graces
- Daily Readings
- Books for Speakers

Activity Books
- Quizzes
- Puzzles
- Painting Books

Daily Readings

Church Stationery
- Notice Books
- Cradle Rolls
- Hymn Board Numbers

Please send a S.A.E. (approx 9" x 6") for the current catalogue or consult your local Christian Bookshop who should stock or be able to order our titles.